How to Grow
FUCHSIA STANDARDS

by
Martin Burley

I.S.B.N 0-9549025-0-5

This book is published by Martin Burley.
Designed and printed by Mitchell & Wright, Printers Limited, of Southport.

DEDICATION

This book is dedicated to the memory of the Local Government Officers and Council Members of Wigan, Crewe, Irlam and Salford for allowing me to enjoy a long career working in public parks.

ACKNOWLEDGEMENTS

I wish to thank the following friends for assisting me with this book:

Jenny Lawson who encouraged me to record my gardening experiences

Jean Kehoe and Louise Clough who patiently typed the handwritten drafts

Eric Unsworth, Geoffrey Oke and Jim O'Reilly for proof reading and offering technical advice

Stan Berry and Peter Blay who made old photographs more presentable

Sheila Draper for scanning my drawings

Phillip Barker and Chris Dixon for photographing the plants

I would also like to thank the staff at Learndirect Patricroft, Eccles, Manchester who are teaching me keyboard skills. The staff of Mitchell & Wright Printers Limited for designing and printing my book.

Finally, my wife Evelyn for her support throughout

CONTENTS

INTRODUCTION 4

SECTION ONE   **PREPARATION** 5

                                         POSITIONING 6

                                         NUMBERS 14

                                         SELECTING PLANTS 17

                                         MATERIALS 19

                                         PROPAGATION UNITS 21

SECTION TWO   **SEASONS**...23

                                         SPRING...24

                                         SUMMER 33

                                         AUTUMN 37

                                         WINTER 39

SECTION THREE   **GROWING SKILLS**...43

                                         WATERING 44

                                         POTTING...48

                                         TRAINING 52

                                         CANES AND TIES.....................................57

                                         FEEDING..61

                                         PESTS AND DISEASES 62

INDEX OF CULTIVARS 63

INTRODUCTION

This book has been written to answer the many questions raised regarding the growing of fuchsia Standards and to encourage gardeners to grow some for themselves. It contains sufficient detailed information to allow the first-time grower to produce fuchsia Standards without the need of previous experience or the use of any automatic growing facilities. Many simple sketches have been used to help the reader and to explain more clearly how the different operations are carried out.

Some of the cultural methods described apply to many other types of garden plants grown in pots as the same principles apply when taking cuttings, potting, watering, feeding and training. However, some of the growing techniques explained may be different from the ones commonly practised by other gardeners. The inexperienced gardener is therefore advised to experiment a little with the growing methods and compare the results before allowing any particular method to become a routine practice.

Each of the growing stages, from the rooting of the cuttings to the development of a full flowering head, presents an interesting challenge. The training of the plant to grow a straight stem and form a well-balanced head are activities which can prove to be fascinating.

The gardener wishing to grow fuchsia Standards will need to look ahead and be prepared to care for the plants each day throughout the growing season. In addition to the normal duties when caring for plants being grown in pots, the plants will need to be trained and the young stems tied to a cane to protect them from being broken.

It is not possible to say how long it will take to grow a Standard plant, as there are many factors which will affect the plant's rate of growth. However, a gardener with reasonable growing conditions can expect to grow a Standard from a cutting within one year. There are four types of Standard to be grown: the Mini, Quarter, Half and Full.

The facilities which will be required will depend upon the numbers and sizes of the plant to be grown. The gardener who wishes to root cuttings in August will need a heated greenhouse to keep the young plants growing during the winter months. When cuttings are to be rooted in spring, the young plants will need to be grown in warm conditions until May. From May onwards, the plants can be grown outside in the open garden. In the autumn at the end of the growing season, the gardener will need to make available a frost-free room to store the plants throughout the winter months.

A gardener without the use of a greenhouse can grow fuchsia Standards by purchasing young plants or whips in April and keeping them protected from frost in a sheltered position in the garden.

The British Fuchsia Society Measurements

To help the gardener to be able to relate to the different sizes of the plants, the British Fuchsia Society have grouped together fuchsia Standards into four categories based upon the length of the stem. These sizes are determined by measuring from the top of the compost to the lower of the branches which form the head. The names given to each of the four categories, starting with the smallest, are MINI, QUARTER, HALF and FULL. The smallest recognised Standard stem is 15cm. The longest is 105cm. Each category is a continuation of the previous size.

Type of Standard	Minimum Length	Maximum Length
MINI	15cm	25cm
QUARTER	25cm	45cm
HALF	45cm	75cm
FULL	75cm	105cm

SECTION ONE

Preparation

POSITIONING 6

NUMBERS 11

CULTIVARS..............................12

SELECTING PLANTS 17

MATERIALS.............................19

PROPAGATION UNITS...........21

POSITIONING

Before starting to grow Standards, the gardener should imagine how they would look in the garden when they have been grown. A good plant will have a well-shaped head growing upon a straight stem, which will enable the flowers to be seen from all angles. To make the most of the Standard plants, they should be positioned at focal points where they will flower throughout the summer months.

The sizes of the plants to be grown should correspond in scale to the size of the garden. Too many large plants being grown in a small garden will result in the head of the plant losing its shape as the foliage growth increases. Small types of Standards being grown in a large garden will be out of proportion and the overall effect of the plant's shape and flower will not be fully appreciated.

When Standards are to be planted directly into the garden soil, the distance between the plants should be considered carefully. The gardener will need to allow for the growth of the head, as the plant will remain in the same position until the autumn. Plants, when grown in pots or containers, can be moved from one location to another as the growth develops. Moving plants around in the home and garden should be done to create interest and to take advantage of the different growing conditions.

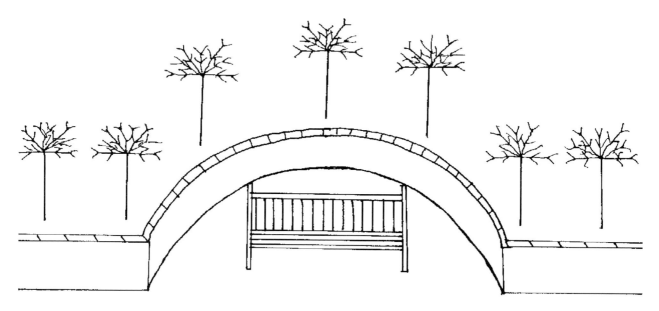

Fuchsia Standards planted directly into the garden soil of a raised bed. The cultivars with long cascading flowers are seen to the best effect when viewed from below. Recommended cultivars: Carmel Blue, Coachman and Miss California.

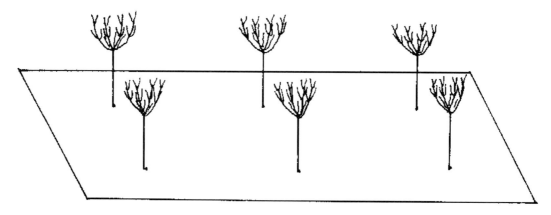

Six fuchsia Standards used as dot plants in a formal flower bed. The extra height lifts the head above the ground cover plants. Only top quality plants of even size and shape should be used to give the desired effect. Cultivars with flowers which grow upright are more popular in these locations as the blooms can be viewed from above. Recommended cultivars: Estelle Marie, Pink Fantasia, Waltz Jubelteen.

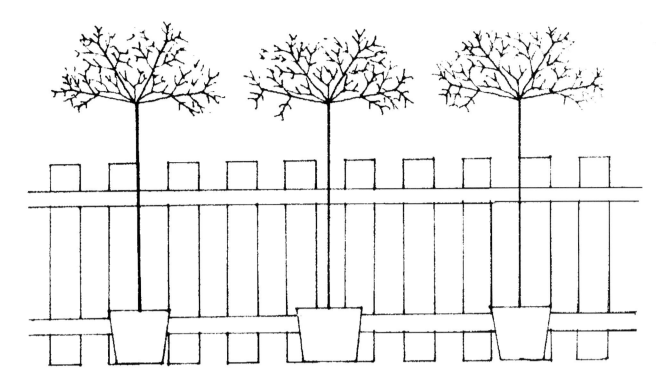

Large Full Standards growing alongside a fence. The well-shaped flowering heads will be appreciated by neighbours. The plants can be grown in pots or planted into the garden soil. In exposed locations, the stems of the plants will need to be tied to the fence to avoid wind damage. Recommended cultivars: Beacon, Shelford and Snowcap.

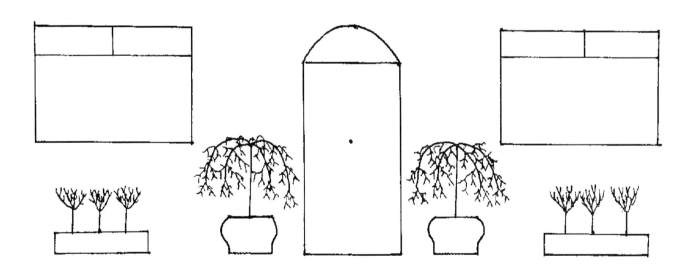

Mature Standards with different growth habits being grown in ornate containers. The plants will need to be turned occasionally to keep the head well balanced.

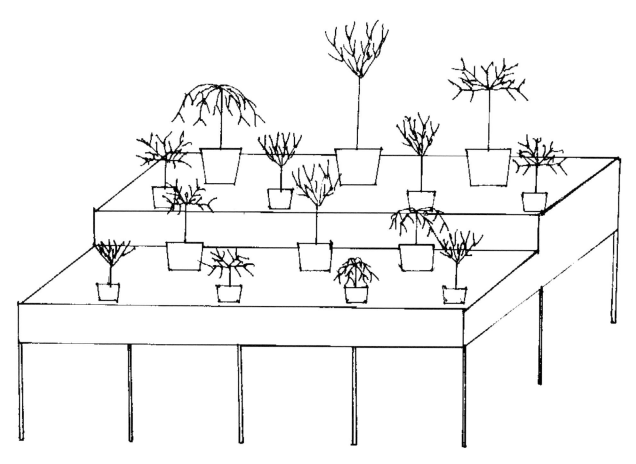

Collection of Mini and Quarter Standards with different head shapes displayed in a cool greenhouse or conservatory. These small plants are easily moved to other parts of the home or garden.
Recommended cultivars: Anita, Briar Lee, Harry Gray, La Campanella, Midas and Patio Princess.

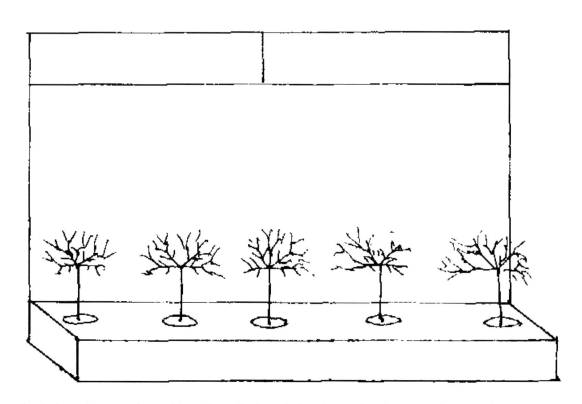

Standard plants in pots plunged into the soil of a window box. The plants can be turned to produce even growth or exchanged with other cultivars as the season progresses.

A DISPLAY OF FUCHSIAS GROWING IN THE AUTHOR'S GARDEN, AUGUST 2004

The hanging baskets arranged upon an ornamental framework are highly visible. The fuchsias Standard in front of the hanging baskets are a mixture of shapes and sizes positioned to allow the natural growth of each cultivar to develop.

Quarter Standards growing in pots on green coloured decking. Each plant has been positioned so that the flowers and growth habit of each cultivar can be fully appreciated.

(See individual cultivars over).

A selection of six-month-old Standard plants grown from cuttings taken in March and flowering in August of the same year. The plants will continue to flower until taken indoors in the autumn.

Jack Shahan

Pink Fantasia

Sir Matt Busby

La Campanella

Rose Fantasia

Patio Princess

Harry Gray

Irene Sinton

Variegated Vivienne Thomson

NUMBERS

Having decided to grow fuchsia Standards, the gardener will need to decide how many to grow. The number of plants should be considered carefully, as each person's interest will differ and the growing facilities which are available will need to be taken into account. **Growing too few plants can be considered as a lost opportunity to gain valuable growing experience, whilst growing too many may result in some of the plants being neglected.**

The gardener with limited growing facilities who wishes to grow only one Standard plant can choose from a straightforward Quarter Standard grown from a Bush cultivar or the more difficult Full Standard grown from a Trailing type.

One Quarter Standard. Ideal for the gardener with limited growing facilities who is growing a Standard for the first time. Select a cultivar with Bush type growth which will grow a straight stem and will branch readily to form a balanced head.

Recommended cultivars: Border Queen, Loves Reward and Midas

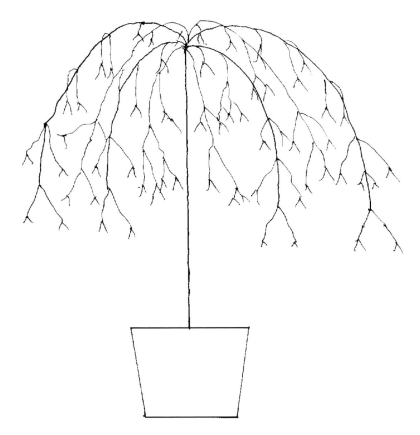

One Full Standard. For the gardener who likes a challenge. Train the Trailing type of fuchsias into a Full Standard. The stem will need to be tied frequently to keep it growing straight. Young shoots growing from the centre of the head will need to be 'thinned' to force outward growth.

Recommended cultivars: Dark Eyes, Eva Boerg and Swingtime.

An interesting exercise is to grow one plant of three different cultivars which have distinctive shapes and are vigorous growers. These plants when trained to become Full Standards will show clearly the variations in growth habits.

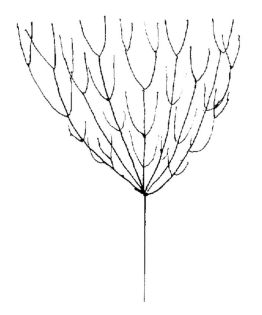

UPRIGHT

Upright cultivars often tend to produce a cone-shaped head, narrow at the bottom, gradually widening out as the growth develops. To control the upright growth of the plant, the young shoots will need to be pinched frequently.

Although the Upright cultivars produce a straight stem quickly, the shaping of the head can prove to be difficult when they are being trained

Recommended cultivars: Chang, Checkerboard and Pacquesa.

BUSH

Bush type cultivars will break naturally and often produce many shoots from the centre of the head. To produce a large head as is required when a Full Standard is being grown, many of the shoots starting to grow from the centre will need to be removed to direct the growth outwards. When the gardener is satisfied the required size of the head has been reached, shoots can then be allowed to develop from the centre of the head

Recommended cultivars: Beacon, Display and Shelford.

TRAILING

The Trailing cultivars need to have the young shoots forced outwards at the initial stage of head training. This is achieved by selecting four vigorous shoots and removing all other shoots as they appear until the selected shoots are approximately 15cm. When this length has been reached, the tip of the young shoots can be removed to allow side shoots to develop and trail naturally.

Recommended cultivars: Dark Eyes, Eva Boerg and Swingtime.

The gardener who is not particularly interested in the growing of fuchsia plants but would still like the challenge of training the plants into the shapes of Standards could grow one each of the four sizes: Mini, Quarter, Half and Full.

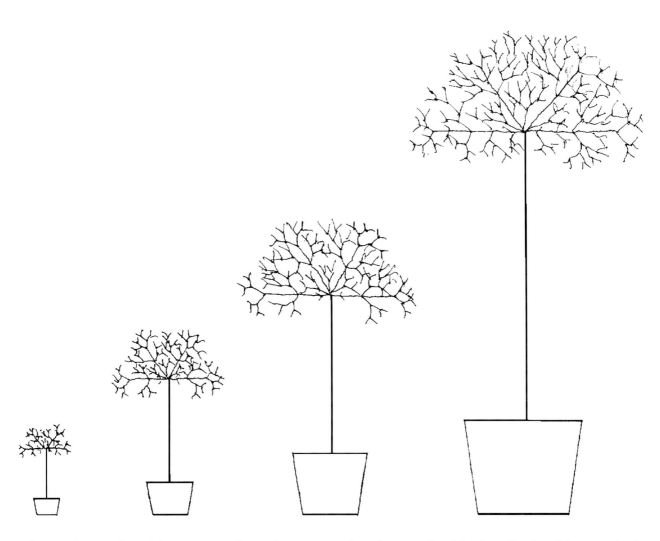

The gardener who wishes to grow four plants, one of each type, should select Bush cultivars, which can be trained to provide a well-shaped head to be kept in proportion to the length of the plant stem and the size of the pot. The least vigorous cultivars should be chosen for the smaller types and the more vigorous ones for the larger types.

Recommended cultivars:	*MINI STANDARD:*	*Babette, Baby Bright, Maria Landy.*
	QUARTER STANDARD:	*Border Queen, Loves Reward, Midas.*
	HALF STANDARD:	*Display, Helen Fahey, Pattie Sue.*
	FULL STANDARD:	*Beacon, Checkerboard and Shelford.*

CULTIVARS

Before deciding upon the cultivars to be grown, the gardener should study a selection of fuchsia catalogues. These can be obtained from specialist fuchsia nurseries and will have lists of those which are considered to be the most suitable to be grown as Standard plants. The catalogues will have photographs of the flowers and give details of the growth characteristics of each variety, i.e. Upright, Bush, Trailing, etc. Photographs of the most popular cultivars can be seen on websites.

The gardener who is inexperienced in growing fuchsias is advised to select cultivars which are considered easy to grow: those which will grow a straight stem and branch naturally to form a well-shaped head. The colour, size and shape of the flowers will also need to be taken into consideration. The chosen cultivars should be tolerant to changes in weather conditions and be resistant to pests and diseases.

The gardener is advised to select carefully and be prepared to shop around to obtain the right cultivars, as they will remain flowering in the garden for many years. If they are being chosen to be displayed at flower shows, then it is worthwhile attending local Fuchsia Society meetings to seek the advice of experienced exhibitors who will be willing to give the names of cultivars which have previously been successful in the various show classes.

Some popular cultivars grown successful as Standards *

Mini Standards
Babette, Baby Bright, Lady Thumb, Little Beauty, Maria Landy, Mini Rose, Paula Jane, Son of Thumb, Tom Thumb, Twinny.

Quarter Standards
Alice Hoffman, Border Queen, Dollar Princess, Estelle Marie, Loves Reward, Midas, Patio Princess, Nellie Nuttall, Purple Pride, Waltz Jubelteen.

Half Standards
Carmel Blue, Celia Smedley, Display, Helen Fahey, Natasha Sinton, Nicki's Findling, Pattie Sue, Pink Fantasia, Turkish Delight, Variegated Pink Fascination.

Full Standards
Beacon, Beacon Rosa, Carla Johnson, Checkerboard, Dark Eyes, Eva Boerg, Shelford, Southgate, Snowcap, Swingtime.

* The 40 cultivars selected have been chosen out of 100 tested by the author over the past ten years. There are many more cultivars available which are equally good, with new ones being introduced each year.

Roy Sinton, one of the county's leading commercial breeders, is seen here passing on his hybridisation skills to his son, Robert. For the fuchsia to remain one of the most popular garden flowers, new cultivers will need to be continuously introduced. A successful cross will bring pleasure to millions of gardeners.

Pollen being transferred from the anthers of one parent onto the stigma of the other parent.

Seed bearing fruit, ripening on the plant.

Four popular fuchsia cultivars bred by Roy Sinton, each with distinctive growth characteristics and suitable to be trained into the shape of a Standard plant.

PATIO PRINCESS
(CAMBRIDGE LOUIE X ESTELLE MARIE A.F.S. No. 2557)

MIDAS
(GRANDMA SINTON X LOUISE FAULCON A.F.S. No. 3345)

PATTIE SUE
(ANN. H. TRIPP X LEONORA A.F.S. No. 3350)

JOHN GROOMS
(COQUET DALE X SHEILA CROOKS A.F.S No. 3960)

SELECTING PLANTS

The gardener, having decided upon the number of plants to be grown and the cultivars, will now need to decide where to obtain the cuttings or young plants from. The more developed the plants are when purchased, the shorter the period of time it will take to train into Standards.

There are four main options open to the gardener:

1. **Take cuttings**
2. **Buy ready-rooted cuttings**
3. **Buy small potted plants**
4. **Buy whips**

Take cuttings

This is the most interesting way to start, providing the gardener has available old 'stock' (See 'Stock Plants' page 24) plants of the required cultivars to take the cuttings from. If this is not the case, then the gardener can purchase young plants from a fuchsia nursery in February and use these as stock plants. If these young stock plants have had the centres of the lead shoot pinched out, the side shoots which develop can be cut off and used as cuttings. If the young plants have not been pinched, then the gardener will need to pinch the centres and await the development of the side shoots to be used for cuttings.

Buy Rooted Cuttings

Many reputable nurseries and mail-order firms will provide ready-rooted cuttings and will have a wide range of cultivars. When purchasing plants in this way, the gardener should inform the nursery or mail-order firm that the plants are required to be trained as Standards and plants which have had the centres pinched out are not acceptable. The centres of these young plants will be trained to form the stem upon which the head will grow. Orders should be placed well before the delivery date and only the selected cultivars accepted.

Buy Potted Plants

The advantage of buying potted plants is that they are more advanced and a gardener can go to the nurseries and select the plants which are the most suitable ones to be grown as Standards. The plants should not have had their centre pinched out and should be free from pests and diseases. It may be necessary to visit several nurseries to find plants of the right quality and cultivar. If all the required cultivars cannot be found, then a recommended substitute will have to be accepted.

Buy Whips

Buying whips is the easiest way to start growing Standards as the plants would be well advanced and the early training done by the nurseryman. The growing tip should be healthy and the stem straight. All of the side shoots and flower buds should have been removed and the cane inserted to keep the plants secure. When growing from whips, the choice of cultivar is limited and the plants may have been neglected prior to being put on sale. The gardener is advised to purchase the plants from a reputable nursery experienced in the growing of whips to be trained as Standards.

Well grown Standard Whips

MATERIALS

The materials required to grow fuchsia Standards are the same as needed to grow other garden plants, i.e. pots, canes, compost, etc. However, as the fuchsia Standards will grow to be taller than the bush types of fuchsias, long canes will be needed to support the head of the plant. If the Standards are to be grown in flower beds, fewer pots will be needed. When they are to be grown on a patio, ornamental containers may be used instead of pots.

Requirements per Plant (to be used as a guideline):

MINI Standard

Potting compost	1 litre
Two pots	0.3 litre and 1 litre
One cane	25cm

QUARTER Standard

Potting compost	2.5 litres
Three pots	0.3 litre, 1 litre, 2.5 litres
Two canes	25cm, 50cm

HALF Standard

Potting compost	5 litres
Four pots	0.3 litre, 1 litre, 2.5 litres, 5 litres
Three canes	25cm, 50cm, 90cm

FULL Standard

Potting compost	10 litres
Five pots	0.3 litre, 1 litre, 2.5 litres, 5 litres, 10 litres
Four canes	25cm, 50cm, 90cm, 120/150cm

Potting Composts

The fuchsia will grow well in the ready-mixed loam, or peat-based composts, which can be obtained in bags from nurseries or garden centres. The choice between loam-based or peat-based is optional. Loam composts retain the moisture longer than the peat-based ones. If a gardener has been successful in using one type of compost, it is better to continue using the same type. A gardener will have become accustomed to watering the plant in that particular kind of compost and will be more accurate when assessing the plant's need for water.

The gardener should purchase composts made by a reliable supplier, as the contents will need to have been mixed to the same consistency and the same type of compost can then be purchased each year.

To calculate the amount of potting compost required, the number of plants to be grown is multiplied by the size of the final pot, i.e.. six Full Standards in 10 litre pots (6 x 10) = 60 litres required.

Pots

Round plastic pots with a good drainage system are recommended. The numbers and sizes will depend upon the type of fuchsia Standards being grown. The pots are re-usable and should be cleaned and stored away after use. Some growers will prefer to grow the larger cultivars of Standards in clay pots, as the extra weight will stabilise them and help to stop them being blown over in windy conditions.

Canes

The number of canes and sizes will depend upon the vigour of the plants and the type of Standards being grown. When the plants are small, split canes are recommended. As the plants grow thick, bamboo canes should be used. When the Full Standards have developed a large flowering head, a strong dahlia cane may be needed for each plant to replace the bamboo cane.

Additional requirements

Rooting compost – the gardener will require a small quantity of rooting compost into which should be mixed 25% of fine vermiculite or perlite to keep the compost open and to help with the drainage. One litre of rooting compost plus 25% of vermiculite will be enough to root 25 average-sized cuttings.

Labels – one white 12cm plastic label for each plant.

String – one ball of 2-ply green string will be needed for tying shoots to canes.

Fertilisers – see 'Feeding' (page 61).

Insecticides/fungicides – see 'Pests and Diseases' (page 62).

PROPAGATION UNITS

There are many types of containers or propagation units which can be used to root fuchsia cuttings. If the gardener only wishes to root a few plants, then a small plastic bag fitted over a pot is all that is needed. If several cultivars are to be grown, then a plastic propagation rooting tray is recommended. Where fuchsias are to be rooted along with cuttings of other garden plants, then a double unit will be suitable. If the gardener grows large numbers of plants and is interested in propagation, then a small automatic mist unit can be used.

From the time when the cuttings are first taken until they are rooted, a temperature of approximately 15°C should be provided. The gardener is advised to place a maximum/minimum thermometer where the cuttings are being rooted and to regularly record the highest and lowest daily temperatures. This will enable the gardener to relate the period of time it takes to root the cuttings to the temperature in which the cuttings are being grown.

SUCCESSFUL PROPAGATION WILL DEPEND UPON AN EVEN TEMPERATURE BEING MAINTAINED

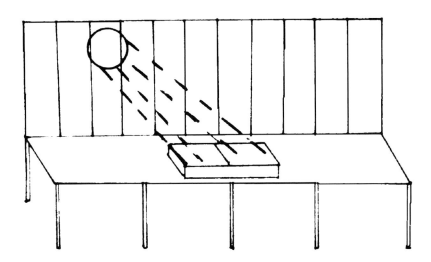

There is the danger of the temperature rising dramatically to kill the cuttings if the sun is allowed to shine through the glass onto propagation units.

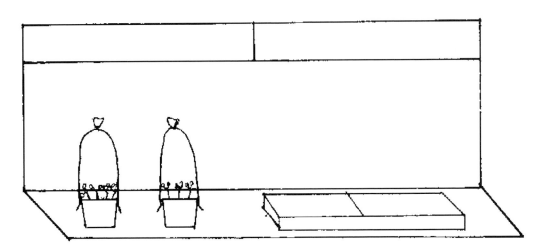

Propagation units in the home will need to have a North-facing aspect.

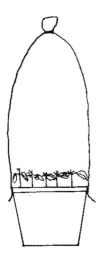

The rooting of cuttings by placing them under a plastic bag has proven to be a simple successful method. The window sill of a North-facing window is a suitable location, as the cuttings will have sufficient daylight without the sudden changes in temperature. When the cuttings have been rooted, they can be moved to a more open aspect within the home. If the cuttings are to be rooted in a greenhouse, then a shady position should be found.

Where several cultivars of fuchsias are to be rooted, a plastic propagation rooting tray with a sliding panel at the top is recommended. The sliding panel can be opened occasionally to allow the air to circulate and to reduce condensation. It can be gradually left open for a longer period when the plants need to be weaned. As was the case when a plastic bag was used, the tray should be positioned out of direct sunlight until the plants have rooted.

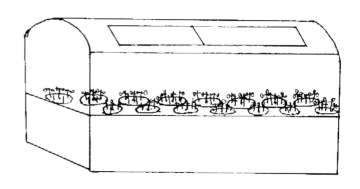

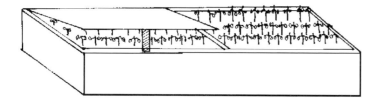

For the gardener who propagates large numbers of plants from cuttings, a wooden unit with two compartments is recommended. The units can be made to the size which will meet the gardener's requirements. By having two compartments with hinged lids or loose panes of glass, the temperature in each compartment can be controlled separately. As the cuttings start to root in the warm section, they can then be moved into the cooler section to be weaned.

For the enthusiastic gardener who is interested in plant propagation, a small automatic mist propagation unit is recommended. Unlike the other types of units, the mist unit normally remains in the same position, as it will be connected to an electricity and water supply. The fine mist spray allows the leaves of the plant to remain cool and moist whilst the underground cable keeps the roots warm. This results in the plant's loss of moisture through leaf transpiration being reduced and the roots

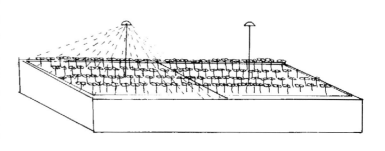

growing quickly due to the extra heat. When using a mist propagation unit, large cuttings can be taken. This will result in the plants growing quickly once they have rooted.

SECTION TWO

Seasons

SPRING 23

SUMMER 33

AUTUMN 37

WINTER 39

SPRING

Spring is the period from February until May, when the shoots on the stock plants start to grow, when cuttings are taken or new plants purchased. It lasts until the young plants have been weaned in the greenhouse before being taken outside.

Stock Plants

Stock plants are the plants from which cuttings are taken. They have been divided into two categories, OLD and NEW.

The OLD stock plants are the ones which have been over-wintered from the previous year and started into growth in early spring. The first cuttings will be taken from the stock plants in early March. Others may be taken from the plants as the shoots develop, until the required number has been reached. The gardener can expect to take approximately 50 cuttings each year from a well grown, free branching stock plant.

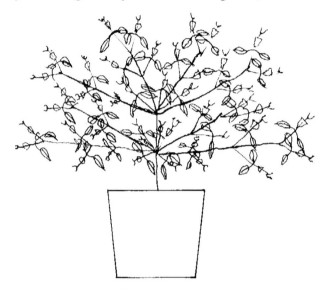

An 'old' stock plant which will branch naturally to produce many cuttings.

The NEW stock plants are the ones which have been purchased from fuchsia nurseries or garden centres in early spring. These new stock plants will have been rooted in the nurseries during the winter months, potted into small pots and be marketed from February onwards.

The gardener should select plants which have had the centres pinched out and have new shoots growing from the sides which can be used as cuttings. Initially, each plant should produce 4 cuttings, with more to follow as the plant develops. All stock plants from which cuttings are to be taken should be healthy and free of pests and diseases. They should not be dry when the cuttings are being taken and any flower buds will need to be removed. Prior to the cuttings being taken, the stock plants should have been exposed to daylight and have been grown in a cool temperature.

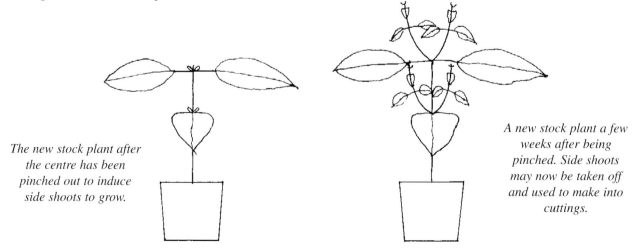

The new stock plant after the centre has been pinched out to induce side shoots to grow.

A new stock plant a few weeks after being pinched. Side shoots may now be taken off and used to make into cuttings.

Cuttings

The rooting of cuttings is one of the most interesting aspects of gardening. Whether it is the rooting of a few plants on a window sill or rooting large quantities using automatic propagation systems, the same sense of achievement will be enjoyed when the cuttings start to root.

The fuchsia cuttings can be rooted at any time during the seven months of the growing season from March until September. The most favourable time to take fuchsia cuttings when the plants are to be trained as Standards is early March before the flower buds start to form. The cuttings taken in March gives the gardener a full season in which to root the plants, train the stem, shape the head and still have enough time to enjoy the plant in flower before the winter months. If gardeners do not have the facilities to root the cuttings in early March, they should not be deterred, as cuttings taken later in the year will make excellent small Standards. Should the gardener only wish to grow the larger Full Standards, the training can continue into the following year.

Taking the Cuttings from The Stock Plants

The taking of the cuttings is the most delicate part of the operation to be undertaken when fuchsia Standards are to be grown. From the time when the young tips are first removed from the stock plants until the time when the cuttings are fully rooted, they should not be neglected. When selecting the most suitable shoots to be cut from the stock plants, the gardener should examine each plant carefully and only remove the minimum amount of foliage to make each cutting. By carefully selecting the cuttings, the stock plants will soon recover and continue to grow more shoots, which can again be used for cuttings if required.

Preparation

A smooth, level working surface will be needed for the making of the cuttings and putting them into the compost. To avoid loss of moisture from the plant's leaves, the work should be done indoors, out of direct sunlight or wind. The compost to be used will need to be of a fine, open texture, warm and moist. Clean 0.3 litre round plastic pots are recommended for rooting small numbers of plants. Each pot will hold six average-sized cuttings.

Making the Cutting

The approximate length of the shoot to be made into a cutting is 6-7cm, the actual length depending upon the cultivar. Each of the young shoots taken from the stock plant should have a soft growing tip and two leaves. If small batches of the same variety are to be grown, the gardener should select shoots of the same size. This will result in the cuttings rooting at the same time and the subsequent plant growth will remain uniform.

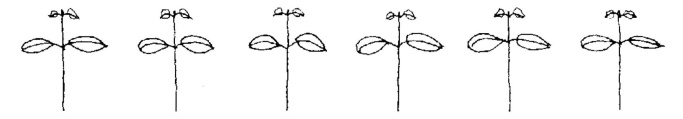

Six cuttings of approximately the same size are taken from the stock plant and trimmed, ready to be placed into the compost. The number of cuttings to be placed into each pot may vary according to the size of the cuttings.

When taking cuttings, the stem should not be handled, the cuttings being held only by the leaves. When removing the cutting from the stock plant, the gardener should place a thumb underneath one of the lower leaves and the index finger under the opposite leaf and then gently move both leaves upwards. Using a sharp pair of small scissors or a budding knife, the stem is cut about 1cm below the lower leaf joint removing the cutting from the stock plant. The next stage is to trim the bottom of the cutting. First, the two lower leaves are cut off as close to the stem of the shoot as possible without damaging it. The next step is to cut off the 1cm of stem which is below the leaf joint. The cutting is now ready to be inserted into the potting compost .

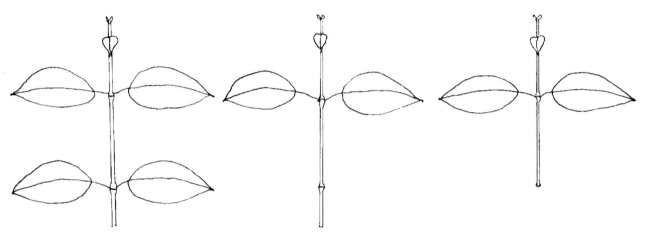

Cutting when first removed from the stock plant.

Two leaves have now been removed.

Bottom of the stem has now been cut back to the leaf joint ready to be placed into the compost.

Vigour of the Cultivars

When making the cuttings, it is often necessary to vary the length of the stem and number of leaves to be left on the cutting, as the vigour of the cultivar and the type of propagation unit being used to root the cuttings will need to be taken into consideration.

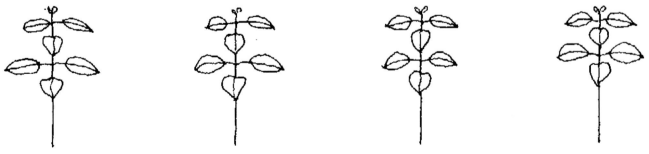

The cultivars being grown as Mini or Quarter Standards are normally slow growing with small leaves and a short distance between the leaf joints. More than one set of leaves will often need to be removed from the stem of the cutting to allow it to fit firmly into the compost. Example cultivars are: Lady Thumb, Lambada, Maria Landy.

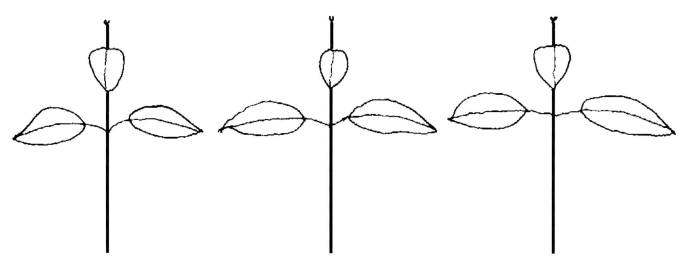

The cultivars with average vigour usually need just two mature leaves on each cutting. These will make good Half Standards or Full Standards. Example cultivars are: Display, Dollar Princess, Snowcap.

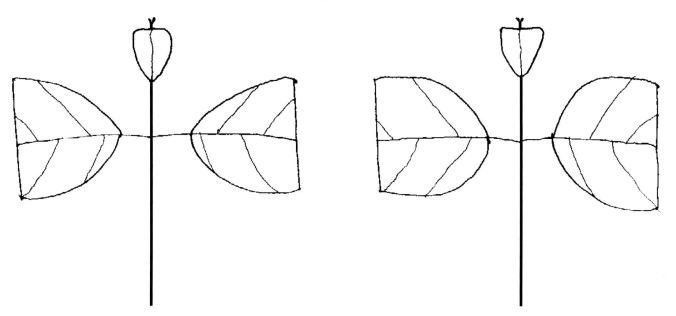

To reduce the amount of space taken up in the propagation unit and water loss through the leaves, vigorous cultivars need only two half leaves on each cutting. Example cultivars are: Chang, Checkerboard, Voodoo.

Placing the Cuttings into the Compost

To prepare for the cuttings, the pots are first filled to the top with compost. The compost is then gently pressed down using the fingers until it is approximately 1cm below the rim of the pot. This space at the top will allow for the plant to be watered without it running over. Using a pencil or small dibber, a hole is made into the compost at the side of the pot to the approximate length of the cutting's bare stem. The cutting is then placed into the hole and the compost gently pressed around it. Care will need to be taken not to bruise the stem or leave any air pockets in the compost. Five more cuttings will then need to be inserted to fill the pot. The pot containing the cuttings should be carefully placed into the propagation unit without dislodging any of the cuttings. Each pot should then be watered using lukewarm water from a can fitted with a fine rose.

The pot is filled with compost and the compost gently pressed down. Using the blunt end of a pencil, a hole is then made into the compost at the side of the pot ready for the first cutting to be inserted.

 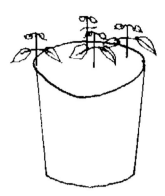 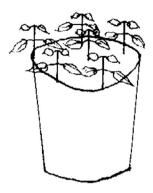

A: One cutting is placed into the compost at the side of the pot and carefully pressed in.

B: Two more cuttings are inserted around the side of the pot and one in the centre.

C: The two remaining cuttings are placed around the sides of the pot.

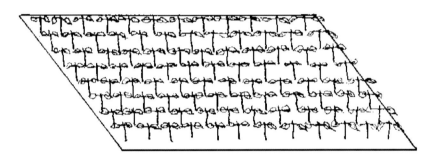

Plastic plug trays can be used instead of pots when large numbers of fuchsia cuttings are being propagated in a mist unit. By rooting the cuttings in trays, the plants are more easily handled and the roots are not damaged when the cuttings are potted.

ADDENDUM

Two-or Three-Leafed Cuttings

The fuchsia plant's natural leaf formation is to have two leaves growing opposite to each other from each leaf joint growing on the stem. However, some cultivars often produce a malformation of the plant's growth, which results in three leaves being formed at each leaf joint.

Many experienced fuchsia growers, when training plants to be grown as Standards, prefer to take cuttings from plants which have three leaves, as there are a number of advantages to be gained. A young plant with three leaves at each joint will be more vigorous. Also, a more compact head can be produced from a three-leaf joint instead of two. The disadvantages when growing plants with three leaves is that they sometimes tend to 'revert back' and start to produce two leaves at each leaf joint, resulting in uneven growth. When Standards are being grown to have a large head, the three-leaf plants have too many shoots at the centre when the growth is required at the outside of the head.

The differences between three-and two-leafed plants is of only minor importance when compared with the overall development of the plant. If a small compact head is required, a three-leafed plant is preferred. If a large head is needed, then a two-leaf plant is preferred. A gardener who has three-leafed plants available is advised to grow some alongside plants with two leaves and compare the results.

WEANING

Cuttings in Propagation Units

Cuttings being rooted under a plastic bag can be weaned by opening the plastic bag for a few days and allowing the air to circulate. The bag can then be cut in half before finally being removed.

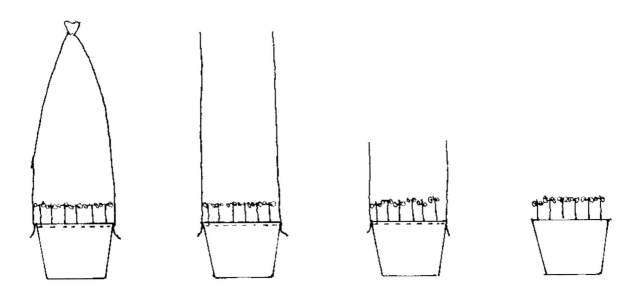

The top of the bag is first opened for a few day's before being cut down to half of its original size. As the rooted cuttings start to show signs of new growth, the remains of the plastic bag are removed.

The first change to be made to the cuttings growing conditions in other propagation units is the gradual removal of the lid of the propagation frame to allow the air to circulate around the cuttings. The gardener should start by opening the lid about 2cm for half an hour each day. After a day or two, the lid can be opened wider and left open for a longer period. This process should continue until the lid can be removed completely. When the lid has been removed from the top of the unit and the cuttings are growing healthily, they are ready to be removed from the propagation unit.

Young plants within the greenhouse

Plants having been rooted in a propagation unit at a temperature of 15ºC in March will need to be weaned if they are to be grown outside in the garden where the temperature can be expected to drop below freezing point during May. In addition to the changes in temperature, the plants will need to withstand winds and exposure to the summer sun. Between the period from when the plants are first rooted in March until they are placed outside in the garden, the plants will need to be moved from one location to another within the greenhouse The changing of growing conditions and the movement of the plants should be done gradually to avoid disturbing the plant's growth. When the plants are first moved to a more open aspect, the leaves may start to droop. If this occurs, the plants can be given temporary protection by covering them with a sheet of newspaper.

The gardener will need to decide when to change the plant's growing conditions If it can be seen that the plants are starting to become weak as a result of being grown closely together, the plants will need to be given more growing space.

(See diagram over)

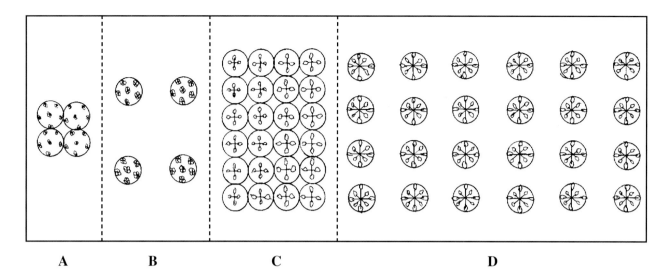

A	**B**	**C**	**D**

A *Four pots each containing six rooted cuttings are placed close together upon greenhouse staging.*

B *As the plants start to grow the pots are separated to expose the plants to more light and air movement.*

C *Each cutting is then potted and placed close together.*

D *When the plants have recovered from being potted and have started to grow they are spaced apart ready to be taken into the garden.*

Taking Plants Outside

It is not possible to give a date when it will be safe for the young fuchsia plants to be taken outside without the risk of the plants being damaged by late frosts. The gardener will need to make the decision depending upon how well the plants have been weaned in the greenhouse and the region where the plants are being grown.

When the plants are being grown under glass in springtime, the temperature can vary from being cold during the night to being hot during the day. To keep a more even temperature in the greenhouse, the ventilators or doors should be closed in the evening and re-opened the following morning. By using a maximum/minimum thermometer, the gardener can record the daily variation in greenhouse temperatures. This information can be used when deciding whether the plants are sufficiently weaned to be moved into the garden.

When the gardener first takes the plants outside, they can be given temporary protection by being placed in a sheltered position and covered using a light plastic material, and later removed to a more exposed location. If the plants are 'touched' by a slight frost, the frost can be washed off by spraying with tepid water early in the morning before the sun shines upon the affected parts of the plants.

Fuchsia cuttings being rooted in a two-bay wooden propagation unit. Six cuttings have been placed in each 0.3 litre pot. Slow rooting cultivars are grouped together and will remain in the propagation unit for a longer period.

When the cuttings are well-rooted, each one will be potted into a 0.3 litre pot and placed close together the greenhouse staging. When they have recovered from the effects of the potting and have started to produce new leaves, the plants will be given more space to allow the growth to develop.

To wean the plants in early May, they are placed outside in an open aspect. If the local weather forecasts predict frost, the plants will be covered with a plastic sheet at night, to be removed the following morning. This process continues until the danger of frost damage is over and the plants can be moved to another location.

Young plants now having been weaned are growing on temporary staging where they will remain throughout the training period. A curtain of nylon netting is lowered to protect the plants during unfavourable weather conditions.

SUMMER

Summer is the time from May until September when the young plants are placed outside and are exposed to the variations of the weather. It is the busy period and the most rewarding period when the fuchsias start to flower.

Weather

The weather conditions in the United Kingdom are favourable for growing fuchsia Standards. Nevertheless, each year, the gardener can expect changes in weather conditions which will cause problems. High winds, long periods of heavy rain and heat waves can damage the plants. To grow successfully, the gardener will need to make the most of the good weather conditions and be prepared to protect the plants when the weather conditions are unfavourable.

Wind damage is one of the main problems when fuchsia Standards are being grown. Large Standard plants with a full head of flowers being grown in an open aspect will need to be protected from strong winds. Wherever possible, the plants should be positioned where natural growth (trees and hedges) will reduce the force of the wind. Plants being grown in an open aspect can be protected by using fine netting to filter the prevailing winds.

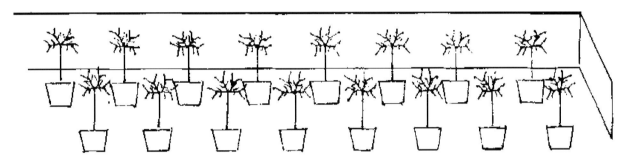

Light nylon netting can be used effectively to protect the plants from high winds.

The normal rainfall expected throughout the summer months is beneficial to the healthy growth of the fuchsia Standard. However, there are times when the rainfall can cause problems. During a long period of rain without any wind movement, the rain water can remain in the dense head of the fuchsia Standard for many days causing the foliage and flowers to decay. If this situation occurs, the heads of the plants will need to be shaken occasionally to allow the water to drain away. Also, a sudden hail shower can tear leaves and flowers in a matter of minutes if the plants are not protected.

During a heat wave, high temperatures and direct sunshine can also cause problems. Large plants growing in pots will 'dry out' quickly and will need to be watered frequently to keep the plants growing healthily. A plant which becomes dry during a heat wave will soon wilt and affect the healthy development of the flowers and growth of the buds. Often, the colour of the flowers will fade and the leaves will scorch. Many pests and diseases flourish in hot dry conditions and will spread rapidly unless treated (see page 62). Extra care will need to be taken when spraying with chemicals during a hot spell. Spraying should be done in the late evening or early in the morning to allow the chemicals to be absorbed before the sun shines on the plants. Any dry plants should be watered prior to spraying.

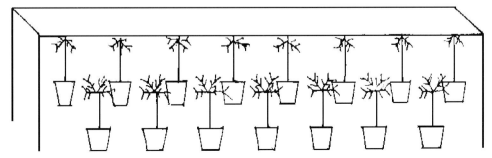

Netting can be used to protect the plants from hot sun or hail showers. Care should be taken when providing protection that the plants do not become weak or the flowers lose colour.

Commitment

Throughout the summer months, May until September, the plants will grow quickly resulting in the gardener being kept busy to avoid the plants becoming neglected.

The examination of the pot plants for the need of water will have to be done each day. (In hot weather, it may be necessary two or three times a day.) During hot spells, the plants will benefit if the under-sides of the leaves can be sprayed with cold water to moisten the atmosphere and destroy potential breeding grounds for pests and diseases.

As the plant's growth develops, the routine jobs of potting, staking and tying will need to be done. A spraying programme using insecticides and fungicides will also need to be undertaken for the control of pests and diseases. The frequency of application will need to be as recommended by the manufacturer of the products. Also, when the plants are in their final pots, they will need to be given plant food in accordance with the growth rate.

While the head is being trained, unwanted shoots and flower buds will need to be removed as they appear. When all of the training has been completed and the head of the plant is in bloom, the old and dead flowers will need to be continuously removed to prolong the flowering period.

(For more detailed information about growing during the summer months see Section Three)

Flowering

Fuchsia Standard plants can be expected to last for many years and will flower from June until October each year. When the plants are to be planted directly into the garden soil, it is important to select a suitable variety for the location, as the plants will remain in the same position until the end of the summer. Cultivars should be chosen which have a long flowering period and will be tolerant to changes in weather conditions.

The care of Standards growing in pots is more time-consuming than when grown in the garden soil. However, there are some advantages to be gained by growing the plants in pots. When the plants start to flower, they can be moved into a prominent position or be moved to a more sheltered position to protect the flowers from damage during unfavourable weather conditions.

For short periods of time, Standards grown in pots can be moved into the home to provide floral displays. Where small Standards are being grown, the plants can be used as table decorations. The fuchsia Standard grown in pots is one of the most popular plants to be seen at a flower show. These plants will have been timed to have the flowers looking at their best on the date of the show, with individual flowers being 'dressed' around the outside of the head to look most effective.

THE ROYAL HORTICULTURAL SOCIETY FLOWER SHOW AT TATTON PARK, CHESHIRE, 18th - 22nd JULY 2001

The author's stand of more than 300 high quality fuchsia Standards, well timed to allow the flowers to open as the five-day show progresses.

Preparing plants. Two weeks prior to the start of the show the Standard plants are placed in an open aspect on the lawn and nylon netting is used to prevent wind damage.

THE EVENT IS A FAMILY AFFAIR

Martin, selecting the ones to be taken to the show.

Evelyn, admiring a full Standard of the cultivar Eva Boerg.

Grandchildren Grace, April and Lewis, loading the small Standards.

Arnold Bishop, family friend who transported all the plants.

Granddaughter, Helen delighted the visitors for the five days of the show.

Evelyn, arranging the plants.

Outside the marquee enjoying a well-earned rest.

AUTUMN

Although the autumn period lasts from September to November, the fuchsia Standard grower has only a few weeks' activity in October when the plants are taken inside to be protected from the frosts.

To protect the fuchsia Standard from frost damage, the plants will need to be taken indoors before the first frosts arrive in the autumn. Prior to being taken inside each plant will need to be HEAD pruned, followed by being ROOT pruned.

Head Pruning

The head pruning should be done in early autumn while the temperature is still warm and the plants are still growing outside in the garden. To prune the head, the growth is first cut back to about half of its original size. The large full Standards are cut back using a pair of shears, the smaller types by using secateurs or a pruning knife. This first 'rough' cut will allow the gardener to see inside the head. The next step is to remove all dead or unhealthy leaves, flowers, buds and old ties, which have remained in the head. The final stage is to remove all weak shoots and shoots which are growing inwards towards the centre of the head and cutting back the remaining shoots so the head is about one quarter of its original size. Any healthy leaves which have remained in the head after the pruning can be allowed to die back naturally before being removed.

The gardener will now be able to see the four branches, which have formed from the four shoots, which were first selected to start the formation of the head (see 'Training' page 54). These four branches will be growing at right angles to each other and will be the basis of a spur type head system, which will develop as the wood hardens and the plant matures.

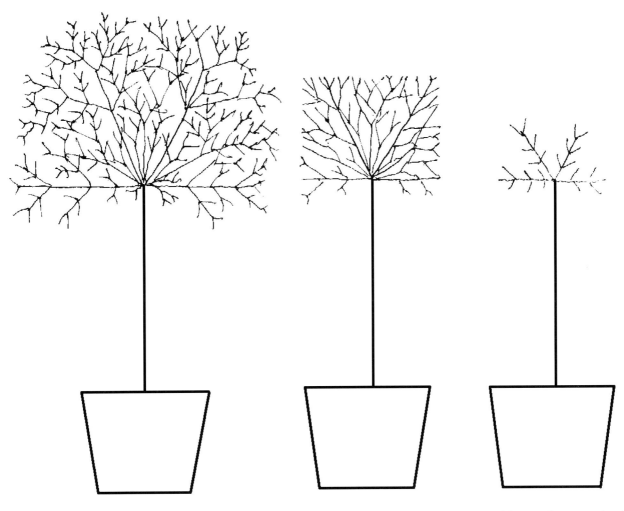

Head of a vigorous Bush Standard before the pruning starts.

Head has been cut back to half of its original size using hand shears.

Head having been cut back again using secateurs or pruning knife. The plant now needs to be root pruned.

After about 14 days, the plants should have recovered from the head pruning and be ready to have the roots pruned prior to being taken indoors for the winter season.

Root Pruning

Plants which have been grown in pots or containers will need to be potted down. These plants should be taken out of their pots, the root system reduced to approximately half of its size and the plant placed into a smaller pot, about half the size of the one which the plant was taken from. Any gaps which appear around the root system should be filled by shaking the plant and pushing old potting compost around the roots. The plants are then watered and the surplus water is allowed to drain away before being taken indoors for the winter months.

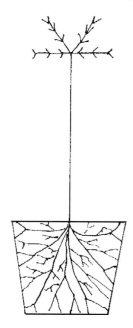

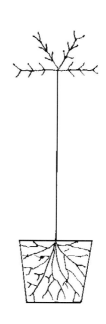

Head has previously been pruned Root system needs to be pruned.

Plant taken out of its pot. Roots cut back to half of original size.

Plant repotted into a smaller pot and watered ready to be taken indoors.

The fuchsia Standards which have been growing in the garden soil with an unrestricted root run will need to be lifted, most of the soil shaken from the roots and the long trailing roots cut off. The plants should then be placed into a pot which is large enough to hold the remaining rooting system using sufficient old potting compost packed around the roots to remove any air pockets; only old 'spent' compost should be used for this purpose.

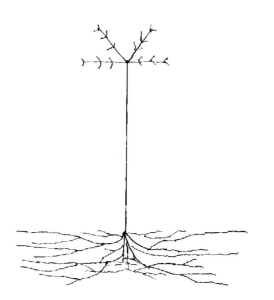
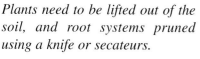

Plants need to be lifted out of the soil, and root systems pruned using a knife or secateurs.

Root system when the plant has been lifted and the roots pruned.

Plant has now been potted and watered ready to be taken indoors.

WINTER

Winter is the time when the plants remain dormant, from October until February. It is the period when a suitable temperature needs to be maintained and the plants watered occasionally.

Frost Protection

Where the grower keeps the plants during the winter months will depend upon the facilities which are available. A frost-free environment where doors and windows can be left open during warm spells for the circulation of air is preferred. The plants can be successfully over wintered in a greenhouse, conservatory, garage or any other rooms where the temperature is suitable. To prepare a greenhouse or other building which is not frost free, the grower should insulate the inside. It is also advisable to have a portable heater available should the temperature drop to near freezing point inside the room during an exceptionally cold spell.

When to take the plants inside will depend upon the region where the plants are being grown and the amount of protection the plant will receive whilst outside. The longer the plants can be left outside without the danger of frost damage, the easier it will be to over winter successfully. The fuchsia Standard will live through the winter months in a dormant state if a temperature of 2°C can be maintained. Keeping the Standards in a warm temperature during the winter is not recommended as the plants will continue to grow and produce weak growth which adversely affects the more natural spring growth of the plant. Plants being over wintered in a south-facing greenhouse or conservatory will be subjected to a wide variation in the temperature when the sun shines through the glass. To avoid this happening, the gardener should use temporary shading or be prepared to ventilate the growing area when the temperature rises.

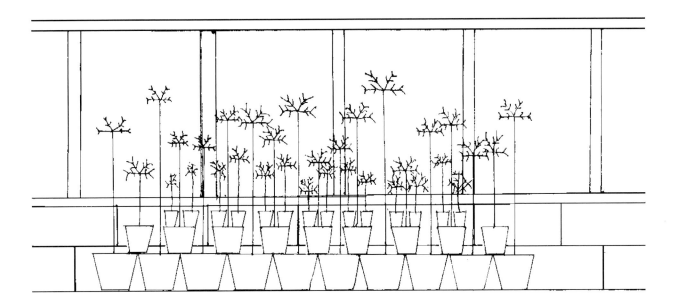

A selection of different-sized fuchsia Standards packed close together in a frost-free greenhouse.
To save space, the small ones can be placed upon larger ones.

Winter Watering

When the head and roots of the fuchsia Standard have been pruned in the autumn ready to be taken indoors for the winter, the plant will need to be thoroughly watered to ensure all the roots and compost are soaked. The watering is best done in the morning to allow the surplus water to drain away before being taken indoors. If the plants remain dormant in a temperature of 2°C, they will need to be examined every six or seven weeks for the need of water. The higher the temperature the plants are in, the more often they will need to be examined for the need of water.

During the winter months, the plants will need enough moisture surrounding the roots to prevent them from drying out completely. The most successful way to check the plant's need for water during the winter months is to lift each plant up and feel the weight of the compost. If the plants feel heavy, they should be left unwatered until they are examined again in another six or seven weeks. If the compost feels light, then the plants should be taken outside to be watered. The watering should be done on a sunny morning and the plants placed in the sunshine to dry before being taken back indoors later in the day.

When the days become longer and the plants are starting to grow again, they will need to be examined more often for the need of water. During the winter months, the atmosphere will need to have been kept dry. In the spring, when the plants have started to grow, a moist atmosphere will be beneficial, with the plants being sprayed occasionally during sunny spells. Whether the plants are watered where they are growing, or taken outside to be watered, will depend upon the growing conditions.

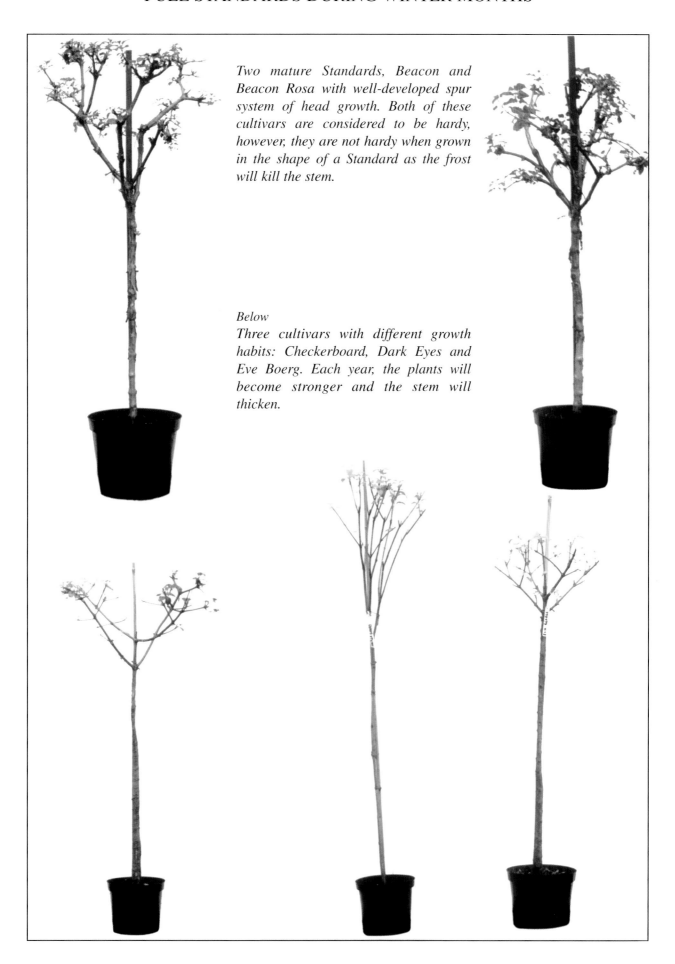

Two mature Standards, Beacon and Beacon Rosa with well-developed spur system of head growth. Both of these cultivars are considered to be hardy, however, they are not hardy when grown in the shape of a Standard as the frost will kill the stem.

Below
Three cultivars with different growth habits: Checkerboard, Dark Eyes and Eve Boerg. Each year, the plants will become stronger and the stem will thicken.

SHELFORD (BUSH) Produces a compact head.

PAQUESA (UPRIGHT) A good example of cone-shaped head, narrow at the bottom gradually widening at the top.

SWINGTIME (TRAILING) Needs to be trained to produce outward growth before allowing the natural downward growth to develop.

SECTION THREE

Growing Skills

WATERING 44

POTTING 48

TRAINING 52

CANES AND TIES 57

FEEDING 61

PESTS AND DISEASES 62

WATERING

It is very difficult to explain when to water fuchsia Standard plants growing in pots without the use of automatic methods as there are many factors which need to be taken into account. To give the plant water at the correct time is often the difference between successful and unsuccessful growing.

Examining Plants
The more often gardeners examine the plants for the need of water, the more accurate they will be in giving the plants water when it is most beneficial. **The period of time between examinations for the need of water is crucial. It is the factor upon which all other considerations are based.**

If the gardener is available to examine the plants at any time of the day, then he/she can water the plants with the knowledge that if there is a change in the growing conditions, which will increase the need for water, the plants can be watered immediately. If gardeners can only look at the plant's need for water occasionally during the day then they will need to decide whether it is most beneficial to the plants to be given water at the present time of examination or leave to be watered at the next time of examination.

When making the decision, the gardener will need to take into account the possible changes in weather conditions which may increase the plant's need for water i.e. increase in temperature or increase in air movement. The adverse effect of giving the plants too much or too little water will also need to be taken into account.

When the gardener is examining the plants for the need of water, it should become a matter of routine to look for signs which will indicate whether the plants are receiving too little or too much water. If the compost becomes light in colour and starts to contract, leaving a small gap between the compost and the sides of the pot, or the leaves at the top of the plant start to droop, the plants are not receiving enough water.

The signs which indicate the plants are receiving too much water are when the compost remains dark and the water takes a long time to drain away. These signs of over watering are often followed by the growth rate of the plant slowing down and the leaves starting to become limp. The plants which are not being watered correctly become weak and are the first ones to be attacked by pests and diseases. In extreme cases, when the watering has become neglected, the bottom leaves will start to turn yellow and the flower buds will start to drop.

Assessment
When only a few plants are grown in small pots, the most accurate way to tell if a plant is wet or dry is to lift it up and feel the weight. If the plant is heavy, the compost is wet and the plant will not need to be watered. If the plant feels light, the compost is dry and will need to be watered. When using this method to tell whether a plant needs to be watered, the 'learner' gardener should take the opportunity to gain experience in assessing the plant's need for water without having to lift up the pot. The gardener should try to judge how long it will take the plant to dry out after being watered, taking into account any changes in the plant's growing conditions.

It is not practicable to lift plants to feel the weight when large numbers are being grown or if the plants are in large pots. Under these circumstances, the gardener will need to rely upon his/her ability to assess the plant's need for water. In addition to considering the period of time between examining the plants for the need of water and the possibility of changes in the plant's growing conditions, the gardener should also take into account other circumstances which will affect the plant's need for water.

Other Considerations
The size of the plant in relation to the size of the pot it is growing in will need to be considered. A large plant with a lot of foliage growing in a small pot will need to be watered frequently. If the large plant becomes dry, the foliage will start to droop and the plant will be susceptible to leaf scorch whenever the sun shines directly upon the leaves. A small plant growing in a large pot will need to be watered less frequently. The water loss through the leaves will be reduced and the large quantity of moist compost surrounding the roots will sustain the plant for a longer period.

The kind of compost which the plants are growing in will have an effect upon the frequency the plant will need to be watered. The heavy loam-based compost will retain moisture longer than the peat-based ones.

The type of pots can also influence the amount of water to be given. Plastic ones will retain moisture longer that the clay ones. Pots with a broad base will retain moisture longer than pots with a narrow base. The number, size and location of the drainage holes at the bottom of the pot will also affect how quickly surface water will drain away. By using the same type of pots whenever the plants are repotted, the gardener becomes accustomed to the period of time it will take for the surface water to drain away and be able to recognise at the early stages any signs of the plants starting to become water logged.

The positioning of the plants in the garden will need to be considered. Plants being grown in an open aspect exposed to sun and wind will need more water than plants being grown in sheltered positions. The gardener should be aware of the sun's movement during the day and when it is likely to shine upon the plants. South-facing aspects will receive the full sun. North-facing aspects enjoy very little sun. East-facing, have the morning sun and West-facing, the evening sun. The gardener should also consider how changes in wind direction will affect the plant's need for more water. An increase in air movement will mean an increase in the plant's loss of water through the leaves.

Misleading Signs
Under certain circumstances, the gardener may have the wrong impression of the plant's need of water.

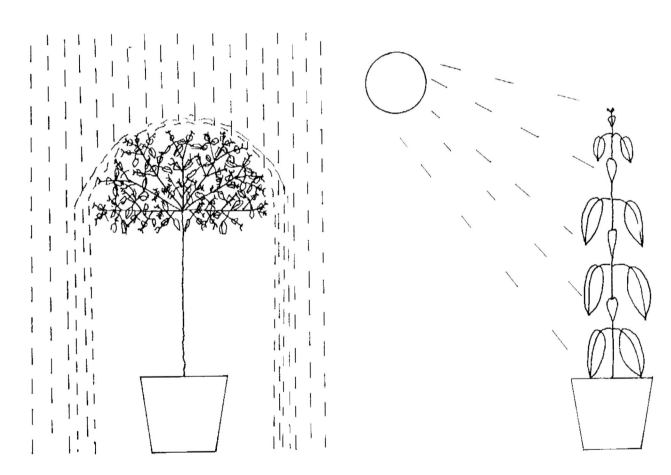

After a heavy shower, the fuchsia Standard with a large dense head often remains dry at the roots whilst the ground around the plant is wet. This is due to the head of the plant forming a canopy which will deflect the rainfall away from the plant's roots.

During a sudden change from cloudy to sunny weather, fuchsia plant's leaves will start to droop giving the impression the plant is dry at the roots and in need of water. Under these weather conditions, the gardener should check whether the roots are dry before giving the plant water as the plant may well droop as a means of saving the water being lost through its leaves.

Rainwater

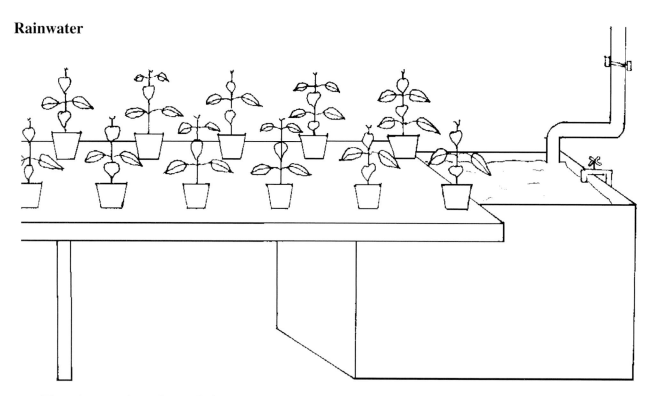

The rainwater from the roof of a greenhouse is drained into an open tank. The water will remain at greenhouse temperature and will contain fewer harmful chemicals than tap water. The water tank should be easily accessible and at a convenient height for everyday use.

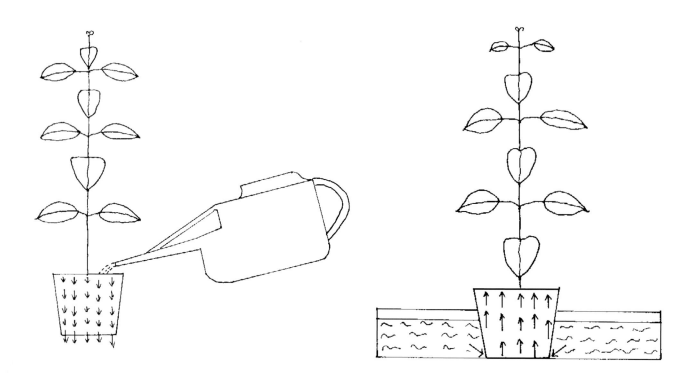

Whenever a plant is watered sufficient water should be given to ensure all of the compost becomes wet. The surplus water which has not been absorbed will drain away through holes at the bottom of the pot.

If a plant had become very dry and the compost has started to contract the best way to ensure all the compost in the pot becomes wet is to place the plant in a container of water for 5-10 minutes and allow the water to soak upwards.

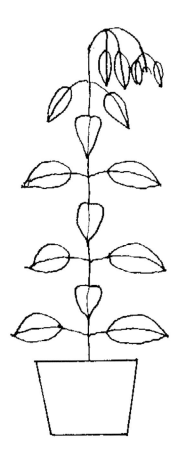

Obvious signs of when the plant is very dry. The shoots and leaves at the top of the plant start to droop and compost starts to contract within the pot.

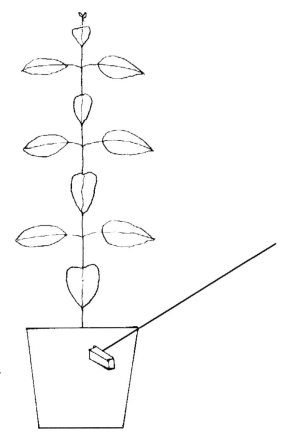

Pot Tapping

When Standards are being grown in clay pots, the best way to tell whether the plant's roots are wet or dry is to tap the side of the pot with a small mallet. If a dull sound is heard then the roots are wet, if a ringing sound is heard the roots are dry. A small mallet can easily be made by drilling a hole into the centre of a piece of hardwood and gluing the end of a 50cm bamboo cane into the hole. Mallet: 7cm x 3cm x 2cm, cane: 50cm.

POTTING

A fuchsia plant growing in garden soil will obtain water and plant food by producing new roots which will travel through the soil to wherever water and plant food can be obtained. When the gardener decides to grow plants in pots, he/she restricts this natural root run and deprives the plant of water and food. To compensate for this loss, the gardener must be prepared to provide the plants with water and food as long as the plants remain in pots. In addition, the gardener should be prepared to provide the plants with more root space to allow the new roots to develop to correspond with an increase in the plant's foliage growth. This is achieved by re-potting the plants from small pots into larger ones.

The number of times each plant will need to be re-potted will depend upon the type of Standard to be grown. During the plant's first season of growth, the Mini Standard will need to be repotted only twice, whilst the Full Standard will need to be repotted five times. If the plants are being grown to be entered into a flower show, then the gardener will need to read the show schedule before deciding upon the size of the final pot, as many of the classes limit the size of pot to be used.

Preparation
Most gardeners will have a potting bench available where the delicate jobs of seed sowing and taking cuttings are undertaken. If the bench is large enough, it can be used for the potting up of fuchsia Standards. The gardener who does not have a potting bench and intends to continue growing plants in pots is advised to make a portable one using light materials. (The bench can then be easily moved and stored away when not in use.)

The gardener should select a place to pot, preferably near to where the plants are growing in a pleasant working temperature with good lighting. The potting bench should be positioned at a comfortable working height without the need to stretch or bend. The bench should be large enough to hold plants, compost, pots, etc. and have a smooth working surface to allow the gardener's hands to pass over without the danger of cuts or grazes. Prior to starting potting, any dry plants will need to be watered and sufficient time allowed for surplus water to drain away. The potting compost should be warm and moist and the pots clean and dry.

Deciding when a Plant is Ready to be Potted
There are no hard and fast rules regarding just when the fuchsia Standard plant will need to be potted. This is a decision which the gardener will need to make depending upon the plant's rate of growth. The gardener will need to delay the potting until the foliage starts to grow out of proportion to the size of the pot it is in. The rooting system should then be examined by knocking the plant out of its pot to see if the roots are well established. If this is the case, the plant is ready to be repotted. If not, then the plant should be left a little longer until the root system has become more established.

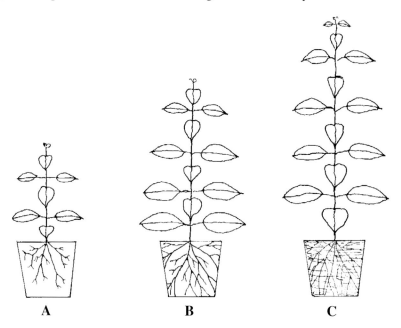

A   *Plant is not ready to be repotted neither the foliage growth or the root system has developed sufficiently.*
B   *Plant is ready to be repotted. When potted at this stage the plant growth will not be disrupted.*
C   *This plant has been neglected and should have been repotted earlier. Roots have become 'pot-bound' which will cause a delay in the development of the new young roots.*

Deciding upon the Correct Size of Pot

The following table gives a suggested potting-up sequence for each of the four types of Standard along with the numbers and sizes of the pots required. The table should only be used as a guideline, as the gardener will be able to decide upon the actual size of the new pot when seeing how vigorously the plant is growing.

Type of Standard	Pot Numbers	Pot Sizes				
MINI	2 pots	0.3 litres	1 litre			
QUARTER	3 pots	0.3 litres	1 litre	2.5 litres		
HALF	4 pots	0.3 litres	1 litre	2.5 litres	5 litres	
FULL	5 pots	0.3 litres	1 litre	2.5 litres	5 litres	10 litres

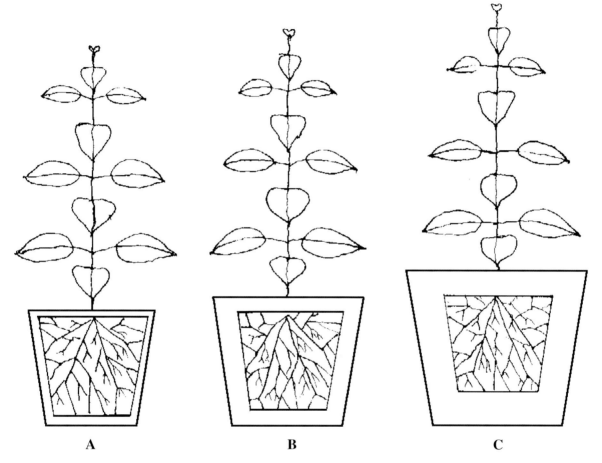

| A | B | C |

A *This shows a new pot which will be too small for the size of the plant's roots. It will result in the plant needing to be repotted in a short period of time.*

B *Shows the correct size of new pot in relation to the plant's rooting system. This size of pot will allow the plant's roots to develop for a reasonable period of time before the plant will need to be repotted or given additional plant food.*

C *This size of new pot will be too large. When the plant is watered, it will remain wet for a long period of time which will result in the growth rate slowing down. The nutrients contained in the compost will have 'leached' away before the plant's roots can absorb the plant food.*

Methods of Potting

The number of times a Standard plant being grown from a cutting will need to be repotted will vary according to the type of Standard being grown. The MINI will need to be repotted twice, the QUARTER three times, the HALF four times and the FULL five times. **Each time a plant is repotted, the two basic principles of placing the plant in the centre and at the correct height always apply.** However, as the plant develops from a small rooted cutting to becoming a large plant, the potting-up methods will need to be changed.

First Potting

The first potting is the most delicate one as it means disturbing newly rooted cuttings and placing them in individual 0.3 litre pots. If there are only a few small roots growing from the base of the cutting, the way to pot is to fill the pot to the top with compost and make a hole in the centre using a small dibber. The cutting is then placed into the hole and the compost carefully pressed around the plant. If the cutting to be potted is well rooted then the pot should be half-filled with compost and the roots placed loosely upon this compost. More compost should then be added until the compost reaches the required height. When potted, the plants should be placed close together in their growing locations and watered. If there is a possibility of the sun shining directly upon the newly potted plants, they should be covered with a single sheet of newspaper until they have recovered from the effects of being potted.

Second Potting

The second potting is from a small 0.3 litre pot into a 1 litre pot. The plant will now have an established root system, which will not be disturbed during repotting.

An example of the second potting

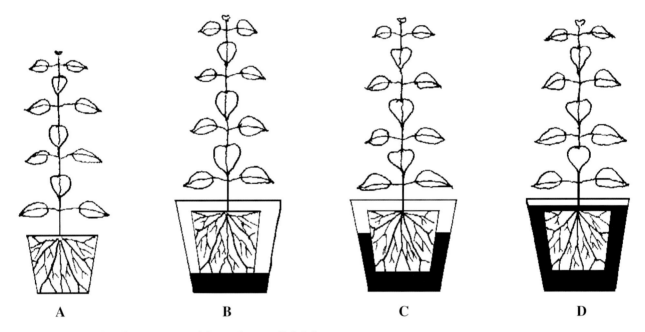

A   B   C   D

A   *The plant has been removed from the small 0.3 litre pot.*

B   *An estimated quantity of compost is placed at the bottom of the larger 1 litre pot. The plant is then placed in the centre of the 1 litre pot resting upon the compost. If the amount of compost at the bottom of the pot does not raise the plant to the required height, then more compost will need to be added. If the plant, when placed upon the compost, is too high then some will need to be removed. When the gardener is satisfied the plant is at the required height and is at the centre of the new pot, more compost will need to be added.*

C   *To add more compost, the plant is held in position with one hand and the other hand is used to add more compost between the plant's roots and the sides of the pot.*

D   *When sufficient compost has been added to hold the plant in position, the hand holding the plant can be removed and more compost added until the whole of the plant's rooting system is covered. The compost can then be gently firmed and the plant watered.*

Third Potting

The third potting is from the 1 litre pot to a 2.5 litre pot The same potting procedures should be followed as when potting from the 0.3 litre pot into the 1 litre pot (second potting). However, now that the plant will be stronger, the compost will need to be pressed more firmly into the pot.

Fourth Potting

The fourth potting is from a 2.5 litre pot into a 5 litre pot. The same principles apply as previously described when potting from a small pot into a larger one. As the 5 litre pot is deep and a large amount of compost will be needed, the potting method will need to be changed. A potting stick will need to be used to press the compost firmly between the plant's rooting system and the sides of the pot to hold the plant upright.

The rounded end of the potting stick is used to press down the compost which has been placed at the bottom of the large pot. The plant to be potted is then removed from the pot it has been growing in and placed upon the compost in the centre of the large pot. The gardener then places the palm of one hand upon the rim of the pot and holds the stem of the plant in position between the index finger and the second finger. With the other hand he/she will 'feed' the compost between the plants rooting system and the side of the pot and firm the compost using the wedged end of the potting stick. As one section is filled, the pot is turned and more compost added. The process of pressing compost between the roots and the side of the pot continues until all of the space has been filled around the roots and the side of the pot and the compost now covers the whole of the plants rooting system. The plant should now be watered and placed where it is to be grown.

Using a Potting Stick

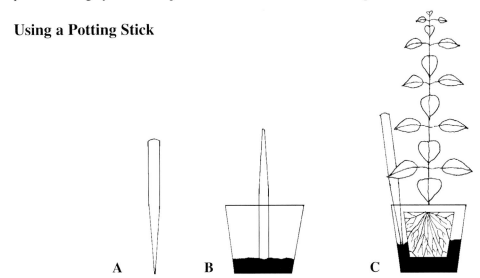

A   *Potting stick made from the shaft of an old garden tool, i.e. spade or fork. Measures 20/25cm rounded at one end and wedge shaped at the other*
B   *Round end of potting stick used to firm compost at the bottom of the pot.*
C   *Wedge-shaped end used to press compost between the roots and sides of the pot.*

Fifth Potting

The fifth potting is from a 5 litre pot into a 10 litre pot. Only the large, vigorous growing Full Standards will be potted into this size of pot. The same method of potting applies as was described in the fourth potting. As the size of the pot and the amount of compost is greater, a larger potting stick may need to be used to press the compost firmly around the roots. The Full Standard will grow to be a large shrub, so any extra compost packed into the pot will help to provide additional nourishment and stabilise the plant. Care will need to be taken when pressing the compost to ensure the roots are not damaged or the compost becomes too compact.

Final Pot

Whichever size of Standard is to be grown, the most difficult of the pot sizes to decide upon is the FINAL pot. The plant will remain in this size of pot for a long period, until the end of the growing season. During this time, the head of the plant will become much larger and the plant will flower. This means the gardener will need to estimate the growth of the head and take it into account when deciding upon the size of the final pot. If the size of the pot which is chosen is too small, the plant will become 'top heavy' and will need to be watered frequently to keep the compost moist. If the size of the pot is too large, the base of the plant will be out of proportion to the length of the stem and the size of the head. There is also a danger of a plant in a large pot remaining wet for long periods. This reduces the rate of plant growth and can lead to the plant's roots starting to rot.

TRAINING

It will normally take three to four months to train a fuchsia plant into the shape of a Standard. The training begins when the first side shoots are removed from the leaf axils of the stem and ends when the last pinch is made to the head to allow the flowering shoots to develop. To explain the methods to be used, this section has been divided into two parts:

    a) Training the Stem   **b) Training the Head**

Stem Training

The training of the stem is relatively simple: it is a matter of growing a shoot to a predetermined length. To do this, all side shoots growing from the leaf axils on the stem will need to be removed as soon as they are large enough to be handled without tearing. This will result in all of the plant's foliage growth going into the lead shoot. The removal of the side shoots is usually done by pinching; however, some cultivars tend to tear easily and shoots should be cut out using a small pair of sharp scissors. Any flower buds or shoots growing from soil level will also need to be removed as they appear.

When the plants have grown two sets of leaves beyond the minimum length of stem, the growth tip should be pinched to complete the stem training. Four shoots should then be allowed to develop from the leaf axils at the top of the stem to start the formation of the head.

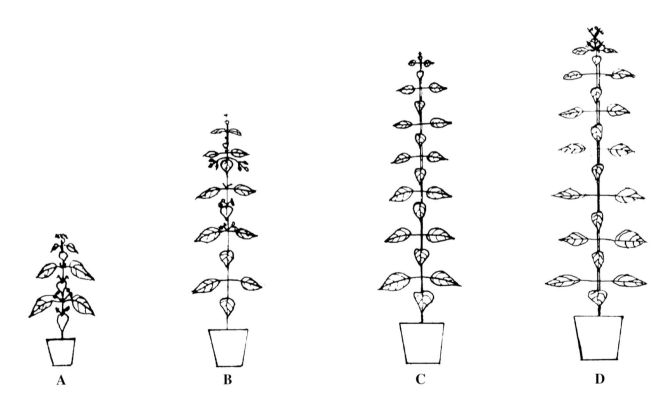

      A   B   C   D

A Side shoots growing from leaf joints need to be removed.

B New side shoots and flower buds will need to be removed as they appear.

C When the lead shoot has grown to the required length, the stem training has been completed.

D The lead shoot has now been pinched and four side shoots allowed to develop. These four side shoots start the formation of the head.

Head Training

The training of the head is more difficult than the training of the stem, as there are three important factors to consider: SHAPE, SIZE and GROWTH HABIT.

Shape - The training of a plant to have a balanced head starts when four shoots, which have grown as a result of the stem being pinched, are selected to form the foundation of the head. These four shoots should be growing at right angles to each other in the shape of a cross. The shoots will need to be chosen from leaf joints which are growing next to each other upon the stem. This will result in a more even growth rate being produced. All other shoots should be removed as they appear, to induce the four shoots to grow outwards and away from each other. When these four shoots have grown to the required length, the tips can be pinched to allow more shoots to develop from the lower leaf joints. (See page 54).

Size - The head will need to be grown in proportion to the length of the plant stem. Slow growing cultivars with small leaves and flowers are more suitable for the Mini and Quarter Standards. The vigorous, fast-growing cultivars with large leaves and flowers, are best for the Half and Full Standards. To produce a small, compact head, all shoots growing from the centre will need to be pinched frequently to restrict outward growth.

To produce a large open head, selected shoots will need to be allowed to grow outwards until the required size is reached, whilst all other shoots growing from the centre of the head will need to be removed. When the head training has been completed, the size of the head will be further enlarged by the growth of flowering shoots. Provision for this additional growth should be made to keep the plant in proportion.

Growth Habit - Most of the popular fuchsia cultivars grown in the shape of a Standard have one of three types of growth: UPRIGHT, BUSH or TRAILING!

The UPRIGHT cultivars, when allowed to grow naturally, tend to produce a cone-shaped head, narrow at the bottom and wide at the top. These cultivars will need to be pinched frequently to produce shoots growing from the centre of the head.

Cultivars with BUSH growth are the easiest ones to train. They will produce many shoots growing from the centre of the head, which can be pinched or thinned to form the required size and shape of head.

Cultivars with TRAILING habits often produce uneven growth which can make training to produce a formal shape of head more difficult. To control the uneven growth, the shoots growing in a downward direction should be removed so that only the ones growing outwards remain. When these shoots have reached the required length, the tips should be pinched and the natural trailing growth allowed to develop.

An example of how a variety which branches freely will need to be trained to form a large, well-balanced head. The head will need to be pinched on three separate occasions.

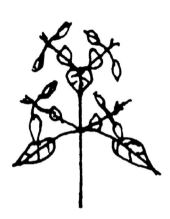

STAGE I

The first pinch has been made to the top of the lead shoot, resulting in four side shoots developing from the two sets of lower leaf joints.

STAGE II

The four shoots which previously developed have now been pinched, resulting in 16 shoots developing.

STAGE III

The 16 shoots have been pinched and 64 allowed to develop. The training of the plant has now been completed. Shoots and flowers can be allowed to grow naturally.

A selection of one-year-old FULL STANDARD plants, each with a distinctive growth habit. For the best results, the training methods will need to be modified according to each cultivar's growth characteristics.

ANITA (BUSH) Difficult to train to produce a balanced head.

ANNABEL. (TRAILING) Stem and head will need to be tied often to keep the growth under control.

BEALINGS. (UPRIGHT) Prolific flowering head. Should be pinched at the early stages of head formation to control upward growth.

BREEDERS DELIGHT (BUSH) Is easily trained as it breaks readily to form a well-shaped head.

CARLA JOHNSON (BUSH) Vigorous growth habit. Needs to be pinched more often than most other bush types.

CARMEL BLUE (BUSH) Loose growth. The long cascading flowers are should be viewed from below to be fully appreciated.

DANCING FLAME (TRAILING) *Difficult to train to produce a formal shape After the initial training it is better allowed to develop naturally as its trailing habit is a special feature.*

ESTELLE MARIE (UPRIGHT) *Needs to be pinched frequently to produce a dense head. A distinctive characteristic of this cultivar is the outward growth of the flowers.*

MADELEINE SWEENEY (BUSH) *Vigorous cultivar. Needs to be pinched early to control growth.*

MISS CALIFORNIA (TRAILING) *Should be tied frequently to keep the stem growing straight and the head growth under control.*

PURPLE PATCH (BUSH) *Easily trained to produce a well-shaped head. During the flowering period, this cultivar is better grown in the shade to avoid the flowers losing colour.*

TURKISH DELIGHT (UPRIGHT) *Needs to be pinched frequently to grow a compact head.*

CANES AND TIES

The fuchsia, when being grown as a Standard plant, will need to be tied to a cane to keep the stem growing straight and to protect the head from wind damage. The number of canes required for each type of Standard will vary depending upon the size of the plant to be grown. The MINI Standard will require the use of one cane, the QUARTER two canes, the HALF three canes and the FULL four or five canes. (Cane sizes can be seen under the heading 'Materials'.) The gardener is advised not to use fewer canes of larger sizes, as this tends to result in the plants falling over too easily. To tie the plant to the cane, the gardener is advised to use two-ply soft green string, or any other type of thin tying material which will blend with the plant foliage and not damage the stem.

Tying the Stem

The number of ties needed to keep the plant growing straight will vary depending upon the growth habit of the plant. **All ties should be made with the intention of stopping the stem from growing away from the cane rather than pulling the stem to the cane.** When tying near to the growing tip of the young plant, it is advisable to tie loosely. This will allow the string to rest upon the leaves and move upwards as the plant grows. A loop-tie is all that is required to keep the stem growing alongside the cane.

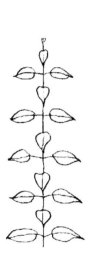
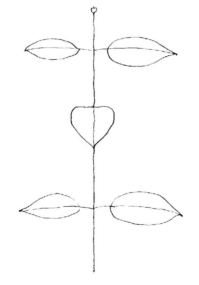
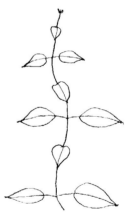

Bush type of growth with close leaf joints will need tying whenever the stem starts to move away from the cane. Example cultivars: Beacon, Display, Dollar Princess.

Upright growth will require only a few ties until the stem reaches the required height. Example cultivars: Chang, Checkerboard, Voodoo.

Trailing growth often needs to be tied at every leaf joint to keep the stem straight. Example cultivars: Annabel, Dark Eyes, Pink Marshmallow.

Cane Replacement

To start supporting the young stem of the plant, a small cane is first inserted into the compost near to the plant's stem and then the stem is tied to the cane. As the plant grows upwards, further ties are made to hold the plant near to the cane. When the growth of the plant reaches near to the top of the cane, the small cane will need to be replaced with a longer cane. Whilst the small cane is still supporting the plant, the larger cane is inserted into the compost near to the plant and the stem is tied to the larger cane. When the gardener is satisfied the plant is being fully supported by the larger cane, the ties holding the plant to the smaller cane can be cut away and the small cane removed. This process of replacing small canes with larger ones continues until the plant reaches its full height.

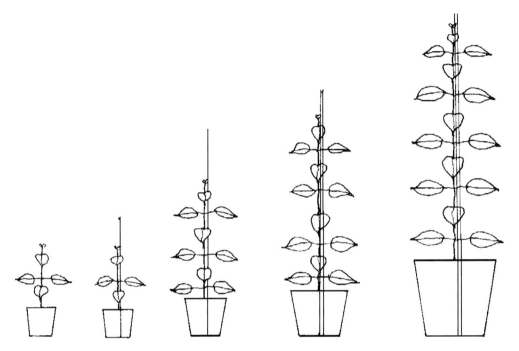

As the plant grows, the smaller canes are replaced with larger ones.

Wrapping the Stem

To give the young stem of a large Standard plant extra protection and keep it growing straight, the stem and cane can be bound together. To bind the stem, a white five-centimetre stretch bandage which has been dyed green is used. The bandage will improve the appearance of the plant by hiding the cane from view and it will also reduce the numbers of unwanted side shoots which grow upon the stem. As the stem grows and swells, the bandage will stretch without causing any damage. After the first season of growth, the bandage will start to rot, eventually dropping from the stem as the plant reaches maturity. Before starting to wrap the stem, the old leaves growing upon the stem will need to be removed. To do this without tearing the stem, the leaf 'blades' are cut from the leaf 'stalk' leaving the stalks upon the stem to die back naturally. It will usually take about two weeks for the leaf stalks to fall from the plant. If they have not fallen after this period, they should be carefully removed by hand.

 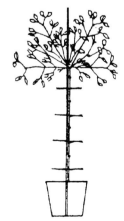 

A *Now that the head is well developed, the leaves will need to be removed from the stem.*　　**B** *The leaf blades have been cut away leaving the leaf stalks attached to the stem.*　　**C** *The leaf blades have either fallen off or been removed. The stem and cane can now be wrapped together.*

58

Tying the Head

The number of ties to be made to support the head will depend upon the type of Standard being grown. The MINI and QUARTER Standards with small compact heads will require very few ties. The HALF Standards with large heads will need to be tied regularly as the plant growth develops. The head of the FULL Standard can be expected to grow to be one metre wide, bearing hundreds of flowers. Extra care will need to be taken to protect these large plants towards the end of the growing season. It is wiser to provide more ties than are needed rather than have the head damaged at the final stages. In later years, when the stems have grown thick and have formed a spur-type of head system, the number of ties needed may be reduced.

The first four initial ties to the head are the most important; without these ties the young branches are likely to break at the point where the branches and the top of the stem meet. Cultivars with large double flowers are the most likely to break at this point, particularly in wet and windy weather when the flowers are heavy due to the rain.

During the first year, when all of the growth is soft, the number of ties to be made will increase to correspond with the size of the plant's head. A series of ties will need to be made to connect the main shoots to the cane. Tying the shoots in this way allows the gardener to improve the appearance of the head by positioning the shoots where they are most beneficial to produce a balanced head. Flowers and leaves should be 'dressed' to hide any unsightly long length of exposed string.

Head Ties

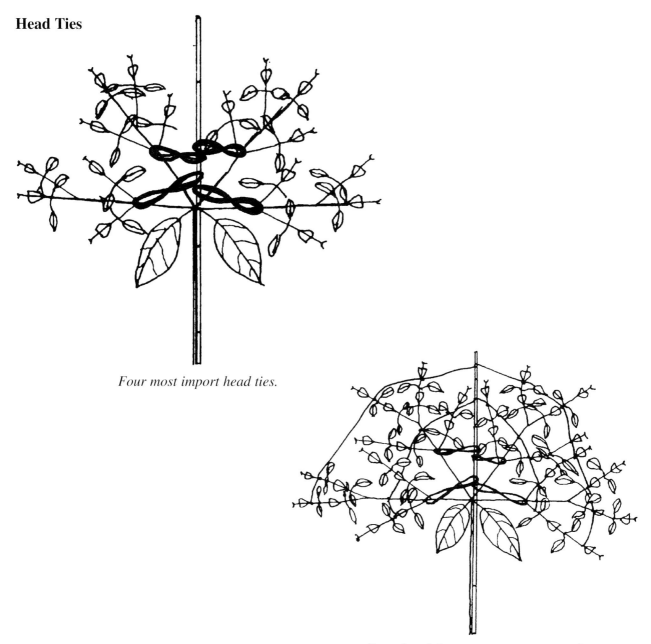

Four most import head ties.

Extra head ties to support new growth.

Methods of Securing Large Standards

When large Standards are being grown in exposed positions, it may be necessary to provide additional supports. The methods to be used will vary according to the locations of the plants.

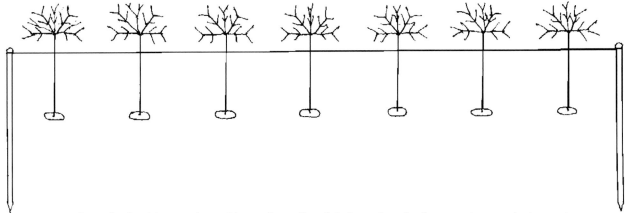

Row of standards with pots plunged in garden soil and tied to a length of green wire attached to stakes.

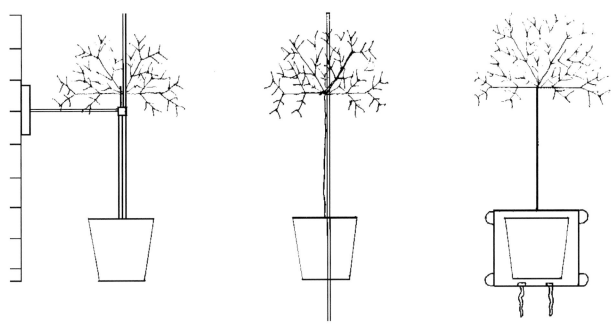

Plant growing upon hard surface near to a wall or fence can be supported using a wall bracket.

Plant growing upon a soft surface can have a stake driven through the plastic pot and into the subsoil.

Plant growing in a container on a hard surface can have the container bolted to the ground.

How to support plants being grown on decking

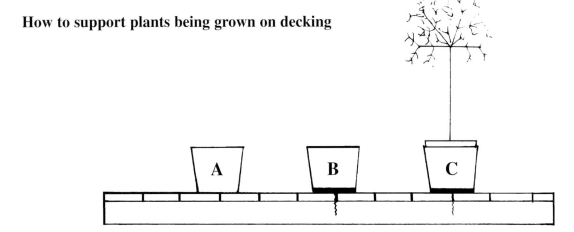

A *An empty plastic pot of the same size the Standard plant is growing in.*
B *A screw, fitted with a large washer is screwed through the bottom of the plastic pot and into the joist of the decking. A small quantity of gravel is then placed at the bottom.*
C *The Standard plant is placed into the empty pot on top of the gravel. The gravel keeps the two pots apart and allows the plant to be turned.*

FEEDING

The recommended way to feed plants is to repot them into larger pots using new compost. The plant food in a good quality potting compost will contain all the nutrients needed to produce healthy growth and the chemicals will be released gradually to correspond with the plant root and foliage growth. When the plant food in the compost starts to become 'spent', the plant will have grown to be larger and will again need to be potted into a bigger pot, thereby providing additional plant food in the compost. This process of repotting is continued until the plant is transferred into its 'final' pot.

When the plant has become established in its final pot and the roots reach the side, the gardener can now start to feed the plant by watering it with a balanced soluble fertiliser. In this instance, the manufacturer's application rates and frequency of application should only be used as a guideline. The gardener examining the plant on a daily basis is in a better position to decide whether the plant is in need of more or less food. If the plant growth starts to become soft and weak, it is a sign of too much nitrogen. Shady and sheltered growing areas tend to result in soft growth, whilst open, windy aspects often result in stunted growth. The application and frequency rates will need to be considered along with the plant's growing conditions and the prevailing weather conditions.

Another method used to feed plants when they are established in the final pot is to apply slow-release pellets or granules to the compost. Although this method is more convenient than using soluble feed, the gardener does not have the same amount of control over the quantity of feed the plants receive. If the growth rate of the plants has been 'checked', they can be given a boost by an application of a foliar feed. This method should only be used as a short-term measure until the plant's growth rate returns to normal.

When the flower buds start to appear, the gardener should change from a balanced fertiliser to one which is high in potash. This will improve the quality of the flowers and harden the stem of the plant.

PESTS AND DISEASES

Prevention

To reduce the risk of plants being damaged by pests or diseases, they will need to be carefully cultivated at all times. Plants, when grown at the correct temperature, given water when needed, potted and fed at the most beneficial times will be resistant to attack from pests and diseases.

Only cuttings taken from healthy stock should be rooted and any new plants should be examined carefully for signs of pests or diseases. If the gardener has any doubt about the health of new plants, they should be isolated and treated until the gardener is satisfied they are pest and disease free.

Throughout the year, any debris or decaying materials should be removed from the growing area to destroy potential breeding grounds. A routine winter cleaning programme should be undertaken: greenhouses, frames and surroundings should be sterilised in readiness for the spring growing season. Plants should be examined on a daily basis for signs of damage or infection. Whenever the weather is warm, the undersides of the leaves should be sprayed with cold water to deter would-be pests from breeding. Mild pest attacks can often be controlled by washing away pests as they appear.

Fungal diseases often attack plants which are being grown in poor conditions or are suffering as a result of bad cultural practices. When a disease is noticed at an early stage, the gardener should reconsider where the plants are being grown and identify any failure in the growing methods.

Cure

The most common pests which attack fuchsias are aphids, white fly and red spider mite. The most common fungal diseases are botrytis, mildew and rust. There are many pesticides and fungicides available at garden centres which kill or control these common pests and diseases. The gardener should follow the instructions issued with the product and follow the application rates, safety precautions, etc. Only the products of well-established firms should be used and only small quantities purchased to ensure there has been no deterioration in quality. By buying small quantities, the gardener can alternate with other chemical products should the pests or diseases become immune to a specific chemical.

If good growing conditions are provided and the plants are sprayed periodically with a fungicide, the fungal diseases which attack the fuchsia plant should not present a serious problem to the grower.

The most difficult problem which faces the gardener is being able to control the pest which damages the plants before the gardener realises they are present. The most troublesome and destructive of these is the vine weevil. The first sign of the presence of the vine weevil is when small bite marks appear on the edge of healthy growing leaves. The weevil will then lay its eggs in the compost and the young grubs which develop will eat the plant's roots, causing the plant to die. It is only at this late stage when the damage has been done and the plant collapses does the gardener realise that the grubs have eaten the roots. Fuchsia growers have been trying for many years to control the vine weevil using chemicals and nematodes, with only a limited degree of success. At present, there is no specific product or method of control which can be recommended and it remains an ongoing problem. However, there are some ways of keeping minor attacks under control.

Whenever the plant is attacked, all of the compost should be removed from the plant's roots. The grubs which have been eating the roots should then be destroyed. The old compost and dead plant should be placed in a plastic bag, the bag securely sealed and then disposed of. Also, in the autumn when the plants are being potted down, the gardener should keep a careful watch for any of the vine weevil grubs and destroy them. All of the compost from the affected plant should then be bagged and discarded. A traditional method of controlling insect pests is to trap them by placing a small clay pot filled with straw on its side under the greenhouse staging. The dry warm conditions inside the pots attract many harmful insects such as vine weevil, earwigs, millipedes, etc. (This method may be worth trying but should not be relied upon.)

Other pests which attack the fuchsia plant and cause damage before the gardener becomes aware of their presence are capsid bug and thrip. These attack the soft growing tips of the plant and the damage is only noticed when the young buds start to open. These pests can be controlled by applying a systemic insecticide whenever the first signs of attack are noticed.

INDEX OF CULTIVARS

ALICE HOFFMAN 14

ANITA 8, 55

ANNABEL 55, 57

ANN H TRIPP 16

BABETTE 13, 14

BABY BRIGHT 13, 14

BEACON 7, 12, 13, 14, 41, 57

BEACON ROSA 14, 41

BEALINGS 55

BORDER QUEEN 11, 13, 14

BREEDERS DELIGHT 55

BRIAR LEE 8

CAMBRIDGE LOUIE 16

CARLA JOHNSON 14, 55

CARMEL BLUE 6, 14, 55

CELIA SMEDLEY 14

CHANG 12, 27, 57

CHECKERBOARD 12, 13, 14, 27, 41, 57

COACHMAN 6

COQUET DALE 16

DANCING FLAME 56

DARK EYES 11, 12, 14, 41, 57

DISPLAY 12, 13, 14, 27, 57

DOLLAR PRINCESS 14, 27, 57

ESTELLE MARIE 6, 14, 16, 56

EVA BOERG 11, 12, 14, 41

GRANDMA SINTON 16

HARRY GRAY 8, 10

HELEN FAHEY 13, 14

IRENE SINTON 10

JACK SHAHAN 10

JOHN GROOMS 16

LAMBADA 26

LA CAMPANELLA 8, 10

LADY THUMB 14, 26

LEONORA 16

LITTLE BEAUTY 14

LOUISE FAUCON 16

LOVES REWARD 11, 13, 14

MADELEINE SWEENEY 56

MARIA LANDY 13, 14, 26

MIDAS 8, 11, 13, 14, 16

MINI ROSE 14

MISS CALIFORNIA 6, 56

NATASHA SINTON 14

NELLIE NUTTALL 14

NICKI'S FINDLING 14

PACQUESA 12, 42

PATIO PRINCESS 8, 10, 14, 16

PATTIE SUE 13, 14, 16

PAULA JANE 14

PINK FANTASIA 6, 10, 14

PINK MARSHMALLOW 57

PURPLE PATCH 56

PURPLE PRIDE 14

ROSE FANTASIA 10

SHELFORD 7, 12, 13, 14, 42

SHEILA CROOKS 16

SIR MATT BUSBY 10

SON OF THUMB 14

SOUTHGATE 14

SNOWCAP 7, 14, 27

SWINGTIME 11, 12, 14, 42

TOM THUMB 14

TWINNY 14

TURKISH DELIGHT 14, 55

VARIEGATED PINK FASCINATION 14

VARIEGATED VIVIENNE THOMPSON 10

VOODOO 27, 57

WALTZ JUBELTEEN 6, 14